Spice Story

Dhruv Baker

Illustrated by Clair Rossiter

OXFORD
UNIVERSITY PRESS

Contents

A World of Flavour

Hello! I'm Dhruv Baker and I love cooking delicious, healthy dishes for my friends and family. I was born in Mexico and have lived in India, Spain, Tanzania and the UK, which means I was lucky enough to learn all about the wonderful foods from those countries while I was growing up.

Cooking isn't just about taking ingredients and turning them into dinner. It's about knowing where they come from, how they are prepared for us to use, and at what time of year they are in season and taste their very best.

What excites me most about cooking is using spices. These ingredients come from all over the globe. Most countries have a national dish which includes a flavour that we associate with that place.

How many of these do you already know?

Paprika

Ginger

Turmeric

Cinnamon

cumin

Star anise

4

Nowadays, we can buy any of these spices from a local shop or supermarket, but as we are going to discover, it wasn't always that easy. Many centuries ago, some of these spices were more expensive than gold and were fought over in wars between nations. Can you believe that black pepper and other spices changed the course of the history of the world?

This book will take you on a journey all over the globe. It's about the food you eat now, what your parents ate when they were children, and even about what your grandparents ate when they were children. To know the food of the world is to know the history of the world. And along the way, you're not only going to learn how to cook my recipes, but also how to use these fantastic flavours to invent your own amazing creations. Let's get started!

Chilli

Saffron

Vanilla

Coriander

Black pepper

You Are What You Eat

Many of us eat too much of the wrong food and not enough of the right food. We need to make sure we get as much goodness out of our diet as possible to help our bodies to develop. A balanced diet is essential for this. Aim to get a good mix every day from the six food groups shown in this pyramid.

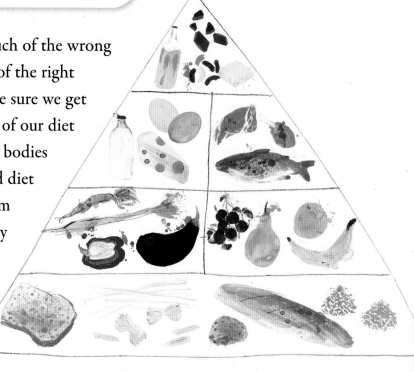

Store Cupboard Ingredients

We can make our cooking much easier by having a well stocked kitchen store cupboard. From these basic ingredients we can create many delicious, healthy and simple dishes.

Fresh ingredients

Eggs
Onions
Garlic
Chillies
Root ginger
Herbs (coriander, parsley, mint)

Sweet ingredients

Sugar
Honey
Vanilla extract (a natural, liquid version of vanilla)

Spice rack

Cinnamon sticks and
ground cinnamon
Vanilla pods
Black pepper, whole and ground
Chilli powder
Ground coriander
Ground cumin
Turmeric powder
Ground ginger
Paprika

Using spices

Drop whole spices into
dishes while they cook and
then take them out before
serving. Or you can turn
whole spices into powder
by grinding them in a
coffee or spice grinder.

Dry ingredients

Rice
Pasta
Couscous
Plain flour
Breadcrumbs
Dried noodles
Dried fruits (apricots, sultanas, raisins)

Pulses

Chickpeas
Kidney beans
Lentils

Other

Stock cubes (chicken and vegetable)
Vegetable oil
Soy sauce
Cling film
Foil
Baking parchment
Freezer bags

Dhruv says ...

Get into the habit of
regularly checking the 'use
by' date on your ingredients
before you use them.

Spice Story: Black Pepper

For thousands of years, Arab traders controlled the spice industry. The use of spices spread from their homeland in the Middle East into Europe. People in Europe came to rely on using spices for cooking, making medicines and preserving food. Most spices were grown in China, Indonesia and India and were then transported overland by donkey or camel and overseas by boat.

Because spices were rare and everyone wanted to buy them, prices rose until a sack of peppercorns was said to be worth a man's life. This meant that European traders wanted to find spices for themselves. In the 15th century, brave explorers began setting sail across the oceans in search of spices. This was the beginning of the Age of Discovery.

These famous explorers all set sail from Spain to find spices, but not all of them got the route right!

1451–1506
Christopher Columbus

Set sail for: India and the Far East

Discovered: The Americas

Brought back: chillies, cocoa, tobacco

about 1460–1524
Vasco da Gama

Set sail for: India (he found it!)

Brought back: nutmeg, cloves, ginger, peppercorns, cinnamon

1480–1521
Ferdinand Magellan

Set sail for: the Spice Islands (called Indonesia today)

Discovered: the passage between the Atlantic and the Pacific Oceans, now called the Straits of Magellan

Brought back: cloves

In Roman times, an **ounce** of black peppercorns could be worth the same as an ounce of precious metals. By the **Middle Ages**, peppercorns were used instead of money to pay rent, **taxes** and **ransoms**!

Once sea routes to India were discovered, Dutch, British, Portuguese and Spanish fleets fought wars at sea to bring home their own 'black gold'.

Do YOU think a pinch of pepper is worth dying for?

Black peppercorns start life as the fruits of this plant, which are picked, cooked and dried.

Fish fingers with black pepper

Ingredients

250g firm white fish (haddock, pollock or cod)

25g plain white flour

2 eggs, cracked into a bowl and whisked

50g breadcrumbs

salt and pepper

1 lemon, cut in half

vegetable oil

Makes: 8 fish fingers
Prep time: 15 minutes
Cooking time: 15 minutes

Be a kitchen professional!

Wash your hands before you start cooking and immediately after touching raw meat or fish. ALWAYS wash anything that has touched raw meat with hot water and anti-bacterial cleaner straight away. Bacteria from raw food can cause food poisoning.

Let a grown-up
cut the fish!

Method

1. Preheat your oven to 200°C/Gas mark 6.
   Cut the fish into fish-finger-sized pieces.

2. Get three bowls. Place the flour into the first
   one, the beaten eggs into the second and the
   breadcrumbs into the third.

3. Mix the salt and pepper in with the breadcrumbs.

4. Toss the fish in the flour and then carefully coat in the
   egg. Finally, coat in the breadcrumbs. This is how we
   breadcrumb or pané the fish.

5. When all the fish is coated properly, brush the fish fingers
   with vegetable oil, place on a baking tray and bake for
   12–15 minutes.

Serve immediately with
a squeeze of lemon.

Ask Dhruv ...

Q: Why do I need to coat
the fish in flour and egg?

A: Flour makes the egg stick to
the fish, then the breadcrumbs
stick to the egg. When the
fish fingers start to bake, the
breadcrumbs form a crust and
the fish steams inside it.

Speak like a master chef!

Pané is a French
word which means
'breaded' (covered
with breadcrumbs).

11

Lamb tagine

Ingredients

Tagine spice mix — mix all of these before you start

1 tsp paprika

1 tsp ground cumin

1/2 tsp ground cinnamon

2 cinnamon sticks

1/2 tsp ground black pepper

1/2 tsp ground ginger

*   *   *

2 tbsp vegetable oil

2 onions, finely chopped

4 garlic cloves, peeled and sliced

500g cubed lamb

1 tin chopped tomatoes

1/2 litre of chicken stock

2 tbsp runny honey

100g dried apricots, roughly chopped

50g raisins or sultanas

1/2 a butternut squash, peeled, seeds removed and cut into 2cm pieces

4 tbsp chopped fresh parsley

1 pinch salt

Butternut squash is super-hard to cut, so let a grown-up do all the hard work!

Makes: Enough for 4–6 people

Prep time: 20 minutes

Cooking time: Approx 2 hours (but for an hour it is cooking by itself!)

Method

1. Preheat your oven to 180°C/Gas mark 4. Heat the oil in a casserole dish and fry the onions over a medium heat for about 10 minutes, until they are soft and starting to turn golden brown. Add the garlic and the tagine spice mix and cook for another 5 minutes.

2. Add the lamb and coat in all the spices. Next, pour in the tomatoes and the chicken stock. Bring to the boil, then cover. Put into your preheated oven for an hour.

3. Remove the lid, stir in the honey, apricots, sultanas or raisins and butternut squash. Cover and return to the oven for another 30 minutes.

4. Stir through the parsley and salt and serve with steamed couscous.

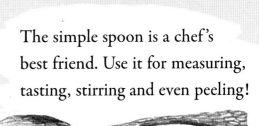

Dhruv says ...

I like to use butternut squash in my tagine but you can use anything you like – carrots are great too! By doing this, you can add a lovely sweetness to a dish without adding sugar.

The simple spoon is a chef's best friend. Use it for measuring, tasting, stirring and even peeling!

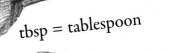

tbsp = tablespoon

tsp = teaspoon

Spice Story: Ginger

Ginger has a warm flavour and can be used in savoury or sweet dishes. But did you know it starts life growing underground as this rather knobbly looking root?

Once you've peeled the ginger root (see my top tip for how to do this on page 17) you can do lots of different things with it.

Slice, grate or chop it up to use in stir-fries and Asian dishes.

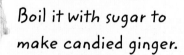

Boil it with sugar to make candied ginger.

Use ground ginger in biscuit dough or cake batters.

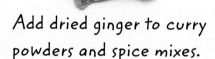

Add dried ginger to curry powders and spice mixes.

Ginger has been used as a medicine for thousands of years. It is said to reduce travel sickness, treat stomach upsets and ease aching **joints**.

The ancient Romans imported it from China and India, but when the Roman Empire fell around 1500 years ago, ginger went with it.

The 13th century Italian explorer, Marco Polo, **revived** people's interest in ginger after he described seeing vast ginger **plantations** on his travels around China.

Just one sheep gets you a whole pound of ginger!

Buy the finest ginger here!

Happily for the traders that came after Marco Polo, rich Europeans were willing to pay high prices for the rare ginger root. As its popularity grew, so did its value.

The Gingerbread Queen

Ginger was a prized ingredient in Tudor times and – believe it or not – gingerbread men may have been invented for Queen Elizabeth I! Apparently, her most important guests would receive gingerbread biscuits decorated to look like them. These would then be eaten at **lavish** feasts.

More gold leaf on the Duke's beard!

15

Thai fishcakes

Ingredients

500g fish (I often use pollock but any
white fish works, or you could use salmon)
1 egg
50ml coconut cream
1 tbsp fish sauce (or soy sauce)
1 tbsp caster sugar
1 fresh red chilli, finely chopped
1 tbsp freshly grated ginger
3 garlic cloves, grated or finely chopped
1 stick of lemongrass, finely chopped
(or the zest of 1 lemon)
5 tbsp fresh coriander
2 tbsp vegetable oil
1 lime

Makes: 8–10 fishcakes
Prep time: 15 minutes
Cooking time: 10–12 minutes

Method

1. Preheat the oven to 200°C/Gas mark 6. Get an adult to place all the ingredients (except the oil and lime) in a food processor and whizz for a few seconds until well mixed.

2. Cover a baking tray with baking parchment. Drop tablespoon-sized dollops of the fishcake mixture onto the paper with space between them.

3. Brush the fishcakes with the vegetable oil, then put into the oven to cook for 10–12 minutes.

4. Serve with a squeeze of lime and some sweet chilli dipping sauce if you like.

Dhruv says ...

These delicious little fishcakes are found all over Southeast Asia, but they always remind me of Thailand. This country's wonderful **cuisine** is made up of five flavours: hot, sweet, salty, sour and savoury (also referred to as 'umami' or the 'fifth flavour'). This dish has it all!

ASK Dhruv...

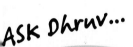

Q: How do I use fresh ginger?

A: Peel the rough skin from the ginger to get to the yellow flesh inside. A teaspoon is easier and safer than a knife, plus it's quicker and wastes much less ginger too! You can then slice or grate as much ginger as you need.

Ginger Recipe 2

Chicken noodle soup

Ingredients

1 tbsp vegetable oil

1 carrot, peeled and cut into small cubes

1 celery stick, cut into small cubes

$\frac{1}{2}$ an onion, finely chopped

200g cooked and shredded chicken

1 litre of chicken stock

3cm piece of ginger, peeled and grated

50g rice or egg noodles

salt and pepper

1 lemon or lime

Makes: Enough for 4–6 people
Prep time: 30 minutes
Cooking time: 20–25 minutes

Method

1. Heat the oil in a large saucepan then fry the carrot, celery and onion for 5 minutes. Add the chicken and stir while frying for 1 minute.

2. Pour in the stock and the ginger and bring the soup to a boil. Add the noodles and simmer until they are cooked.

3. Add salt, pepper and a squeeze of lemon or lime, then serve.

Dhruv says ...

All over the world there are various versions of this dish which people claim are the perfect medicine for when you aren't feeling well. This is my recipe but play around with it using other spices and ingredients until you find your favourite version. I always use the leftovers from a roast chicken but you can also use a couple of cooked chicken thighs or breasts. To make it veggie-friendly, swap the chicken stock for vegetable stock and use 200g of whichever vegetables you fancy instead of the chicken.

Optional extras

Why not try adding some of these ingredients?

2 spring onions, finely sliced

2 star anise

2 tbsp fresh coriander, chopped

1 tbsp soy sauce instead of the salt

1 fresh red chilli, finely sliced

1 small tin of sweetcorn

Ask Dhruv ...

Q: What is star anise?

A: A beautiful, star-shaped spice which has an **aniseed** flavour. It can be used in sweet and savoury recipes.

Spice Story: Chillies

Chillies are part of the pepper family and add heat and warmth to recipes. These flavours are often found in Indian, Asian and Mexican dishes, but this tongue-tingling spice originally came from the Americas after Christopher Columbus found himself there in 1492.

Columbus brought seeds of the chilli plant back to Spain and before long Portuguese traders began to sell it in India and Asia. It is believed that around fifty years after it arrived in Europe, the chilli was being grown nearly all over the world!

In 1912, an American **pharmacist** called Wilbur Scoville worked out how to measure how hot different chilli peppers are. When you eat something with chilli in, it feels 'hot', right? But it's actually not hot at all. Not like a hot cup of tea. Chillies play a trick on your brain ...

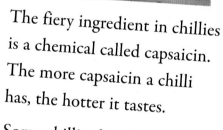

The fiery ingredient in chillies is a chemical called capsaicin. The more capsaicin a chilli has, the hotter it tastes.

Some chillies have very little capsaicin in them, but beware: some chillies are so hot, they explode off the end of the Scoville Scale with a rating of around 2 million SHU (Scoville Heat Units)!

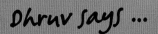

Dhruv says ...
Don't try all of
these at home!

SHU rating	Name
0	Sweet bell pepper
100–500	Pimento
1000–2500	Rocotillo pepper
2500–10 000	Jalapeño
30 000–50 000	Cayenne pepper
50 000–200 000	Bird's eye chilli
100 000–350 000	Scotch bonnet
350 000–450 000	Red savina pepper
Over 1 million	Bhut jolokia (also called the ghost pepper)
Up to 2 million	Trinidad moruga scorpion

Ask Dhruv ...

Q: Help! My mouth
is on fire after eating
spicy food!

A: Drink a glass of milk or eat ice cream
or yogurt. The protein casein in dairy
products sticks to the oily capsaicin. When
you swallow, the capsaicin goes too. If you
can't eat dairy products, chew on bread,
rice or pasta instead to soak up the heat.

Chilli Recipe 1

Chilli con carne

Ingredients

2 tbsp vegetable oil

2 onions, finely chopped

2 garlic cloves, crushed

1 tsp paprika

1 tsp ground cumin

1–2 tsp chilli powder (or 3–4 dried chillies)

500g minced beef

3 tbsp tomato purée

1 tin of chopped tomatoes

$\frac{1}{2}$ litre of chicken stock

2 tins of kidney beans, drained

salt and pepper

Makes: Enough for 4–6 people
Prep time: 15–20 minutes
Cooking time: 1 hour

Method

1. Fry the onions in the oil for 5–7 minutes in a deep saucepan. Add the garlic and cook for another 2–3 minutes.

2. Add the spices and cook for another 2 minutes. Then add the mince and cook it until it turns brown. Keep stirring every couple of minutes for 10 minutes.

3. Add the tomato purée and the tinned tomatoes. Stir for another 2 minutes. Pour in the stock and the kidney beans and bring it to the boil.

4. Reduce the temperature and simmer the chilli without a lid on the saucepan for 30 minutes. Season with salt and pepper. Serve with rice.

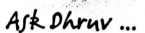

Ask Dhruv ...

Q: What are the rules for cooking raw meat or fish?

Dhruv says ...

This is a quick and easy version of a dish made famous by cowboys in the Wild West. They would have used chunks of meat and they sometimes took it out with them on the range. The version we know today is usually made with mince and kidney beans.

A: Make sure raw meat is cooked all the way through. There should never be any pink meat. If there is, cook it for longer. Use separate chopping boards for raw meat and ALWAYS wash your hands after touching raw meat or fish.

Chilli Recipe 2

⚠️ **WARNING!** This recipe contains nuts.

Chicken stir-fry

Ingredients

2 tbsp vegetable oil

400g chicken breast, cut into 2cm strips

3cm piece of ginger, peeled and cut into matchstick-sized pieces

12 spring onions, cut into 2cm pieces

1 large red chilli, deseeded and finely sliced

2 garlic cloves, finely chopped

4 tbsp soy sauce

2 tsp honey

100g mushrooms, sliced

1 red pepper, deseeded and sliced

1 handful of beansprouts

1 carrot, peeled and cut into thin strips

1 small handful of cashew nuts

200ml chicken stock

juice of 1/2 a lemon

1 tsp sesame oil

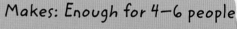

Makes: Enough for 4–6 people
Prep time: 25 minutes
Cooking time: 15 minutes

⚠️ **ALWAYS** wash your hands after touching fresh chillies and **NEVER** touch your eyes afterwards. Otherwise it will really sting!

Method

1. Heat the vegetable oil in a frying pan or wok and add the chicken, ginger, spring onions, chilli, garlic, soy sauce and the honey and stir-fry for 7–8 minutes.

2. Add the vegetables, nuts and stock and stir-fry for another 5–7 minutes.

3. Squeeze over the lemon, stir through the sesame oil and serve with noodles or rice.

Ask Dhruv ...

Q: How do I get the seeds out of a chilli?

A: You need that magical utensil, the teaspoon, again! Use a knife to carefully slice down the length of a fresh chilli from stem to tip. Open it up and use a teaspoon to scoop out the chilli seeds.

Dhruv says ...

The great thing about this recipe is that you can make any type of stir-fry you like! Swap the chicken for prawns, lamb or beef. You can easily make it vegetarian by adding more vegetables or tofu instead of meat, and swapping the chicken stock for vegetable stock. This recipe is the perfect way to use up leftover food and help you eat more veg.

Spice Story: Coriander

Coriander is a really interesting ingredient because it gives us both a herb and a spice – and the two versions taste very different!

Herb or spice?

Herbs come from the leaves of plants.

Mint, parsley, basil and chives are all herbs.

 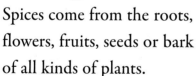

Spices come from the roots, flowers, fruits, seeds or bark of all kinds of plants.

You can eat the stalks and the leaves of a coriander plant – the parts that make it a herb. These are often used in Asian and South American recipes. It adds a zingy flavour to dips such as guacamole and salsa, too!

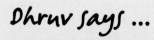

When the coriander berries (its fruit) are dried, they are called coriander seeds. These seeds are ground or used whole as a spice.

In Indian cuisine, coriander seeds are called dhania. They are mixed with other spices such as ginger, pepper and chilli to make curry powders.

A very ancient history of coriander

- The Ancient Chinese believed eating coriander seeds would make them **immortal.**

- Ancient Egyptians placed coriander seeds in the tombs of their **pharaohs.**

- It is possible that the Romans introduced coriander to Northern Europe and Great Britain.

- European explorers took coriander with them to the Americas in 1670, where it became popular in Central and South America.

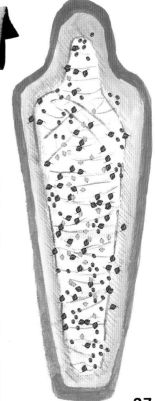

Carrot and coriander soup

Ingredients

2 tbsp vegetable oil
1 onion, finely chopped
1 1/2 tsp ground coriander
1 large potato (Maris Piper or King Edward, for example), peeled and finely chopped
500g carrots, peeled and finely sliced
1 litre of chicken or vegetable stock
salt and pepper
juice of 1 lemon
4 tbsp fresh coriander, finely chopped

Makes: Enough for 4–6 people
Prep time: 15 minutes
Cooking time: 40–45 minutes

Be a kitchen professional!

Keep a bowl for peelings next to you as you work. This will help keep your cooking space clean and tidy. Throw food scraps away all in one go or put them on your compost heap.

Method

1. Heat the oil in a large saucepan and add the onion. Cook over a medium heat for 10 minutes until it's soft and starting to brown or **caramelize.**

2. Add the ground coriander and stir for a couple of minutes, then add the potato and carrots and stir for another minute or two.

3. Pour in the stock and allow to simmer for 20–25 minutes.

4. Blend with a hand blender or in a jug blender. Add salt and pepper and the lemon juice and serve with the fresh coriander scattered over the top. Delicious!

Ask Dhruv …

Q: Why do I need to chop the carrots and potatoes so finely?

A: Cutting these ingredients finely helps them to cook quickly, which means they keep more of their **nutrients.**

Dhruv says …

This is an interesting dish as it uses both the herb and the spice version of coriander together. Can you taste the difference between them?

Soups freeze very well, so make up a whole lot and then freeze portions in plastic containers for a quick and tasty meal.

Vegetarian Curry

Ingredients

Curry spice mix — mix all of these
in a bowl before you start
2 tsp ground coriander
1 tsp ground cumin
1 tsp chilli powder
1 tsp turmeric powder

     *   *   *

2 tbsp vegetable or light olive oil
2 onions, finely chopped
4 garlic cloves, crushed
2 tsp grated ginger
4 tbsp tomato purée
1 aubergine, cut into 2cm cubes
1/2 a head of cauliflower, cut into small florets
2 tins of chickpeas, drained
salt and pepper
200ml water or vegetable stock
juice of 1 lime
small bunch of fresh coriander, finely chopped

Makes: Enough for 4–6 people
Prep time: 15 minutes
Cooking time: 35–40 minutes

Method

1. Heat the oil in a large saucepan, add the onions and cook for 5 minutes.

2. Add the garlic and ginger and cook for another 2 minutes.

3. Add the spice mix and fry for 1 minute, then add the tomato purée and allow to cook for a further 2 minutes.

4. Add the vegetables and cook for 3–4 minutes. Now add the chickpeas, the salt and pepper and the water or stock. Cover and cook for 10 minutes.

5. Stir again and cook with the lid off for another 10 minutes. Add the lime juice and serve with the coriander scattered over the top.

Ask Dhruv ...

Q: What could I serve with this curry?

A: Rice, breads such as naan or chapatis, or eat it as a chunky soup straight from a bowl!

Dhruv says ...

Keep all the veggies the same size when you cut them so they will cook at the same time. This is a good way to practise your knife skills and will help you on your way to becoming a master chef!

Spice Stories: Vanilla and Cinnamon

Vanilla

Have you ever seen a vanilla pod? Look: it's a long, sticky case full of thousands of black vanilla seeds. These pods come from a specific **orchid** which was originally grown in Mexico.

1519 Whilst on an expedition through Mexico, a Spanish explorer named Hernán Cortés discovered vanilla (and chocolate!).

1520s Cortés introduced vanilla to Europe on his return to Spain, but vanilla pods on that side of the world mysteriously failed to grow.

1520s–1830s Nobody realized that the orchid could only be **pollinated** by one type of bee. And that bee could only be found in .... Mexico.

Late 1830s A Belgian **botanist** worked out how to pollinate the orchid – which flowers for only one day – by hand.

Work faster! The world needs more vanilla!

At last, vanilla pods could be grown almost anywhere in the world!

Cinnamon

Cinnamon doesn't start life as that dusty brown powder you find in little jars. This curled-up tree bark is cinnamon too! These **fragrant** sticks were used in perfumes in Ancient Egypt.

During the Middle Ages, the source of cinnamon was a closely guarded secret. Arab traders brought the spice into Europe, but only the wealthiest people could afford to buy it. Having some cinnamon in your store cupboard was a real **status symbol** – the 15th century version of owning the latest mobile phone!

Oooh!

Aaah!

To justify their high prices, cinnamon traders made up tall tales to make this spice seem more valuable. Do you believe that cinnamon could only be found in deep canyons guarded by snakes? Or that enormous birds guarded it inside nests at the top of impassable mountains? I'm not sure I do, but I still love cooking with it!

Vanilla meringues

Ingredients

vegetable oil
5 large egg whites
250g caster sugar
seeds from 1 vanilla pod (or 5–6 drops
of vanilla extract)

Makes: 8–10 large meringues
Prep time: 20 minutes
Cooking time: 2 hours cooking
plus cooling time

Method

1. Preheat the oven to 120°C/Gas mark 1 or 2. Whisk the egg whites using a food mixer or a hand whisk until they are able to form stiff peaks. Turn the speed up and add the sugar one tablespoon at a time, waiting about 5 seconds in between adding each spoonful of sugar.

2. After a few minutes all the sugar will be in and you will have a thick, glossy mixture. Add the vanilla seeds or extract at this point and carefully fold them in.

3. Lightly brush a sheet of baking parchment with vegetable oil. Using a tiny bit of the meringue mix, dab the four corners of the baking parchment and stick it to a flat baking tray.

4. Using a large spoon, dollop the mixture onto the parchment. Depending on the size of meringues you want to make, you may need extra parchment and another baking tray.

5. Cook in the oven for 1³/₄–2 hours. Turn off the oven and leave the meringues inside to cool. (This could take up to 2 hours.)

Serve the meringues however you like! Crush them and eat with ice-cream and fruit. Sandwich two together with whipped cream or dip them in melted chocolate.

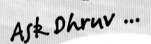

Ask Dhruv ...

Q: How do I use a vanilla pod?

A: Split vanilla pods lengthways with a knife and scrape out the tiny black seeds with a teaspoon.

Dhruv says ...

Don't throw away your deseeded vanilla pods. Put them in a jar filled with plain caster sugar. It will slowly turn into vanilla-flavoured sugar!

Cinnamon Recipe

Chocolate, cinnamon and almond brownies

Ingredients

180g dark chocolate, broken into squares
150g unsalted butter, cut into cubes
200g soft brown sugar
$\frac{1}{2}$ tsp ground cinnamon
200g ground almonds
6 eggs

Makes: 20 brownies
Prep time: 20 minutes
Cooking time: 35–40 minutes

Method

1. Preheat the oven to 160°C/Gas mark 3.

2. Butter a brownie tray and line with baking parchment.

3. Put the butter and chocolate in a glass bowl. Place the bowl over a saucepan of hot water, making sure the bottom of the bowl doesn't touch the water. Heat gently.

Speak like a master chef!

Using a bowl over hot water like this is known as a *bain marie*.

4. When the chocolate and butter have melted, add the sugar, cinnamon and ground almonds and mix well.

5. Separate the eggs very carefully, making sure you don't break the yolks.

6. Stir the yolks into the chocolate mix. In a separate bowl, whisk the whites using a food mixer or hand whisk until they are able to form stiff peaks.

7. Stir a third of the egg whites into the chocolate mixture. Then carefully fold the remaining two-thirds in. To do this, use a few smooth strokes until the whipped egg whites are just combined with the chocolate mixture. When it's ready, pour into the lined brownie tray.

8. Cook in the oven for 35–40 minutes. Remove and allow to cool in the tin before turning out onto a board and cutting into squares.

Dhruv says ...

Make sure NO egg yolk gets into the white. The bowl you whisk the egg white in must be completely dry, clean and free of any grease.

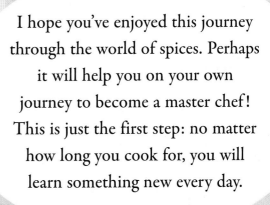

I hope you've enjoyed this journey through the world of spices. Perhaps it will help you on your own journey to become a master chef! This is just the first step: no matter how long you cook for, you will learn something new every day.

Glossary

aniseed: a flavour that's like liquorice

baking parchment: paper with a non-stick surface used in cooking

botanist: someone who studies plants

caramelize: when a food's natural sugars are released and it becomes golden in colour

cuisine: a type or style of cooking from a particular place

fragrant: having a pleasant smell

immortal: able to live forever

joints: places in the body where two parts of the skeleton join together

lavish: grand and luxurious

Middle Ages: the time in history from the 11th century to the 15th century

nutrients: goodness that your body gets from food

orchid: a flowering plant that usually grows in hot countries

ounce: a form of measurement, equal to about 28 grams

pharaohs: rulers in Ancient Egypt

pharmacist: someone who prepares and gives out medicines

plantations: places where plants are grown

pollinated: the transfer of pollen so more plants can grow

ransoms: money paid to release someone being held as a prisoner

revived: renewed something; started it again

status symbol: something that tells other people about your wealth or position in society

tagine: a North African stew which is cooked slowly and made with meat, vegetables and spices; also the name of the pot the stew is cooked in

taxes: money that must be paid to the government or rulers of a land

Index

About the Author

I'm Dhruv Baker and I love to cook! I have always enjoyed making great food for my friends and family and in 2010 I won a TV cookery show called Masterchef.

Cooking is an important skill, but it's also one of the most exciting ways to be creative. I hope that, after reading this book, you'll be inspired not only to cook my recipes but also to invent your own amazing and delicious creations. Imagine surprising your family by cooking them wonderful, exciting food from all over the world! Good luck and have fun!

Greg Foot, Series Editor

I've loved science ever since the day I took my papier mâché volcano into school. I filled it with far too much baking powder, vinegar and red food colouring, and WHOOSH! I covered the classroom ceiling in red goo. Now I've got the best job in the world: I present TV shows for the BBC, answer kids' science questions on YouTube, and make huge explosions on stage at festivals!

Working on TreeTops inFact has been great fun. There are so many brilliant books, and guess what ... they're all packed full of awesome facts! What's your favourite?